EXCEPTIONAL AFRICAN AMERICANS

Neil deGrasse TYSON

Spokesperson for Science

Norman D. Graubart

E **Enslow Publishing**
101 W. 23rd Street
Suite 240
New York, NY 10011
USA

enslow.com

Words to Know

astronomy—The study of objects in outer space.

dwarf planet—A body that moves around the sun. It is smaller than a planet.

experiment—A test used to answer a question or make a discovery.

planetarium—A theater with a giant screen that shows pictures and videos of space.

professor—A teacher at a college or university.

research—Careful study that is done to discover or learn new facts.

science—A way of learning about the world using experiments.

science communicator—A person who makes scientific ideas easy for people to understand.

solar system—The sun and all of the objects that move around it.

universe—Everything that exists.

Contents

Neil deGrasse Tyson

CHAPTER 1

Early Life

Neil deGrasse Tyson was born in New York City on October 5, 1958. He was raised in a neighborhood called the Bronx. Neil's mother, Sunchita, was a scientist who studied aging. Aging means getting older. His dad, Cyril, was the leader of a group called Harlem Youth Opportunities Unlimited. This group helped African-American kids get the chance to have a better life.

Neil's family often visited museums around New York City when he was growing up. One of these museum visits changed his life. When he was nine,

Neil went to the Hayden Planetarium. A **planetarium** is a theater with a giant screen that shows pictures and videos of space. Here he found out that he could learn more about space by studying **science**. Neil is now the head of the Hayden Planetarium himself!

Before he could become a scientist, though, Neil had to do a lot of hard work. He went to the Bronx High School of Science, where he learned more about how people study the **universe**.

Neil Says:

"I look up at the night sky. I don't feel small—I feel large. I feel connected to the universe."

This is the Hayden Planetarium, viewed from the outside. Inside that big ball are a giant screen and theater seats.

Neil deGrasse Tyson is wearing a vest covered in stars. He wears this vest often when he speaks in public.

CHAPTER 2

Student of Science

Neil's life changed again when he was seventeen. He was getting ready to go to college. One day he got a special letter from someone at Cornell University. The letter was from a **professor** named Carl Sagan. In the letter, Sagan offered to show Neil around the university. Neil was very excited.

What was so special about this professor? Carl Sagan was America's most famous scientist in the 1970s and 1980s. Sagan was often on television talking about **astronomy**, the study of objects in outer space. Most importantly, he tried to make this

Carl Sagan holds up a globe in his office. He was interested in more than science, which is why you can see so many books on his shelves.

hard science easy to understand. Imagine what it would be like to meet your favorite sports player or movie star. Now you can guess how Neil felt to walk around with his hero!

Neil Says:

"I already knew I wanted to become a scientist. But that afternoon, I learned from Carl what kind of person I wanted to become."

The First Book

Neil studied at Harvard University and graduated in 1980. He then went to the University of Texas at Austin and Columbia University, where he studied more about astronomy. In 1989, he wrote his first book. It was called *Merlin's Tour of the Universe.*

The book had questions written by people from around the world who wanted to know more about Earth and space. Neil's book answered their questions in words they could understand.

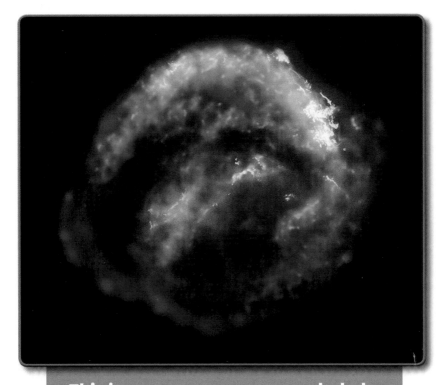

This is a supernova, or an exploded star. Neil studied supernovas during his college years.

CHAPTER 3

Neil's Job

Neil taught college classes while he was studying. Then, after he graduated, he continued to study stars and other space objects.

In 2001, President George W. Bush asked Neil to be part of a group that would think about America's future in space. Neil was one of the only scientists in the group. He helped them come up with a plan for the United States to explore space in the next century. Neil has also worked with other groups that help bring science into the 21st century.

Head of the Hayden

Today, Neil's main job is being the director of the Hayden Planetarium. This is a very important job. The Hayden Planetarium takes information from astronomers and other scientists and makes it easier for other people to understand.

Neil does many things as part of his job. He does **experiments** and **research**. He also helps other researchers. Neil is the voice you hear if you visit the planetarium and watch one of their space videos.

Neil Says:

"I don't think you have to do anything special to get kids interested in science, other than to get out of their way when they're expressing that curiosity."

Neil talks about the latest scientific discoveries to an audience. Neil has become America's most famous science communicator.

This is a great job for Neil because he is both a scientist and a **science communicator**. A science communicator explains big, complicated scientific ideas to people who are not scientists.

Until September 2006, all students were taught that Pluto was a planet in our **solar system**. But scientists began to think that Pluto was actually not a planet. Neil was one of these scientists. This is because Pluto is different from Earth or any of the other planets. It is more like other kinds of objects in outer space. It is now called a **dwarf planet**. Neil got many angry letters from kids when he told everyone that Pluto is not a planet!

Pluto was changed to a dwarf planet because new objects were found in space. They were almost the same size as Pluto!

These people are inside a planetarium watching a video about space. Look how big the screen is!

CHAPTER 4

America's Science Teacher

Being the director of the Hayden Planetarium is hard work. But Neil has also been doing other things to teach Americans about science. He hosts a weekly radio show called *StarTalk*. On this radio show, Neil talks to all kinds of people. He talks to comedians, movie stars, and other scientists. He uses the radio show to make science more popular and fun for the listeners.

Neil Explains the Universe

In 2014, Neil hosted a television series called *Cosmos*. *Cosmos* taught viewers about planets, stars, and also about Earth and life on Earth. In fact, Carl Sagan hosted his own show called *Cosmos* in the 1980s. Neil thought it would be a good idea to do a new version of the same series. Along with Neil's many books, *Cosmos* has helped bring the big universe into our own homes.

Neil drives around in the car that astronauts drove on the moon. He's riding with Eugene Cernan, who is the last American who has walked on the moon.

Neil deGrasse Tyson started his life being interested in the universe. He became a scientist to answer his questions about space. With hard work and some help along the way, he became America's leading science communicator. Now he brings his knowledge to us. Maybe you want to be a scientist one day. If you do, you can learn from Neil about how to reach your goals.

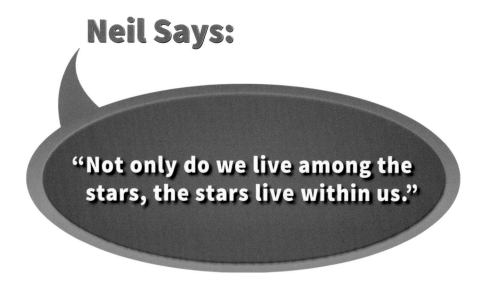

Neil Says:

"Not only do we live among the stars, the stars live within us."

Timeline

1958—Neil deGrasse Tyson is born in New York City on October 5.

1969—Another person named Neil, Neil Armstrong, is the first person to walk on the moon.

1976—Neil graduates from the Bronx High School of Science.

1980—Neil graduates from Harvard University.

1988—Neil marries Alice Young.

1989—Neil's first book, *Merlin's Tour of the Universe*, is published.

1991—Neil gets a doctorate degree from Columbia University.

1996—Neil becomes the Frederick P. Rose Director of the Hayden Planetarium.

2001—President George W. Bush appoints Neil to the Commission on the Future of the US Aerospace Industry.

2006—Neil begins hosting the *NOVA scienceNOW* television show, which airs until 2011.

2009—Neil hosts his first episode of *StarTalk*.

2014—Neil hosts the *Cosmos* series.

Learn More

Books

Coupe, Robert. *Earth's Place in Space.* New York: PowerKids Press, 2014.

Poolos, Christine. *What Is an Object in the Sky?* New York: Britannica, 2015.

Sabatino, Michael. *20 Fun Facts About Galaxies.* New York: Gareth Stevens Publishing, 2014.

Web Sites

discoverykids.com/category/space/
Kids learn about space through fun activities, quizzes, games, and videos.

nasa.gov/audience/forkids/kidsclub/flash/
Includes interactive games, puzzles, and other space-related activities.

Index

Published in 2016 by Enslow Publishing, LLC.

101 W. 23rd Street, Suite 240, New York, NY 10011

Copyright © 2016 by Enslow Publishing, LLC.

All rights reserved.

No part of this book may be reproduced by any means without the written permission of the publisher.

Library of Congress Cataloging-in-Publication Data

To come.

ISBN 978-0-7660-6668-7 (library binding)
ISBN 978-0-7660-6666-3 (pbk.)
ISBN 978-0-7660-6667-0 (6-pack)

Printed in the United States of America

Photo Credits: Getty Images: Cindy Ord/Getty Images Entertainment, p. 1; Santi Visalli, p. 10; Chandra X-ray Observatory/Universal Images Group, p. 12; Earl Mcgehee/Getty Images Entertainment/Getty Images North America, p. 15; Hill Street Studios, p. 17; Stephen Chernin/Getty Images News/Getty Images North America, p. 19; Shutterstock.com: ©Toria (blue background throughout book); ©Helga Esteb, pp. 4, 8; ©Sean Pavone, p. 7; ©Vadim Sadovski, p. 16; Steve Cole, p. 20.

Cover Credits: Cindy Ord/Getty Images Entertainment (portrait of Neil deGrasse Tyson); ©Toria/Shutterstock.com (blue background).